DANIEL JAY GROSSETT

How To Become Streetwise

Simple steps to be confident, assertive, and successful in all situations

First edition

This book was professionally typeset on Reedsy.
Find out more at reedsy.com

Contents

1

Introduction

I was born and raised in South London and lived in many rough areas, like Brixton and Croydon; to me, they were home. Roaming these streets for thirty-five years made me the confident, assertive man I am now. There's no place or crowd I cannot feel comfortable in, whether passing a gang of hooded youths in the street or meeting government officials in the houses of Parliament. I've experienced it all. This book contains advice to help anyone thrive in all situations.

I gained confidence through experience. I've always been reasonably confident, and being the smartest in class as a kid may have fuelled that. But it was also because my mother became an alcoholic and crack smoker when I was ten that surrounded me with situations where I had to be assertive. So from my youth, I had the roughest types of people around me, and that environment became an asset. It forced me to grow fast, integrating with rowdy people from every background.

I have also overcome many inner and outer adversaries, like over-religiousness, perfectionism, drug addiction, homelessness and quitting smoking. I spent over six years in ten different prisons on forty-plus occasions, including harsh environments like HMP Feltham, Belmarsh and Wormwood Scrubs. This gave me crucial people skills. Multiple friends have become murderers, while others have become famous music stars. I also experienced the drug game selling crack and heroin.

I've lost family members, including my best friend and mother, Louise, who was a legendary Brixtonian in her own right whom I learned much from. This made me realise life is too short to spend time being someone we're not. We all want to be the best version of ourselves. And being comfortable in any situation life challenges us is a crucial aspect of self-mastery. Over the years, I've experienced a lot, which has moulded me into a conscientious man ready for anything life throws at me.

Everyone is the same. Yes, we all come from different backgrounds and heritages and are entirely unique, but ultimately, everybody wants to be happy. Whether that's the local drug dealer, hardman or politician. So whoever you come across in your journey, know that, for the most part, they're simply seeking happiness in the way they know how. But our different upbringings, environments and beliefs shape how we find that. So, a street robber wanting financial gain may discover that fulfilment in robbing valuables from his victim. Our aim is to reduce the chances of becoming that victim. And when we possess confidence and assertiveness, the likelihood of us being one deteriorates significantly.

Of course, anyone can be victimised at some point. Even the heavyweight champion could get robbed at gunpoint, but his attributes make that highly unlikely. We'll cover some techniques you can use to put you in a position of power, no matter the situation.

This isn't based upon the basic info available on street smarts, like always carrying a phone, avoiding dark places or ensuring travelling with friends when possible. But, of course, we'll cover such things. Instead, it's about the deeper underlying concepts that, when practised, being comfortable on the streets will certainly not be an issue for you.

I've seen and done a lot, from selling drugs to robbing people to becoming a sought-after barber in every prison I attended. And I've learned valuable skills that are vital for street confidence. If you master them, you'll thrive in all situations.

2

Mindset

Mindset is the basis of most things in life. The first step into assertiveness is a constructive mentality. A crucial component of a robust mindset is knowing what you want and the tangible actions you can take to achieve it. "Someone without direction is already lost," I once read. So, we must have direction and a strong mentality that serves us as a positive asset. Therefore, a healthy mindset and belief in yourself are crucial to being comfortable on the streets and achieving life goals.

To achieve anything, we must first envision it. Then we can work out the necessary steps to achieve our goal. Once we know them, we can work towards success by completing the smaller steps needed. For example, you must use each step to get to the top of the stairs, so simply ensure your footing is correct to get to the next step ahead of you. Before long, you'll have scaled the staircase.

Give yourself positive affirmations and eradicate negative self-talk. We all feel low or doubtful sometimes, but our ability to reaffirm positive emotions helps us overcome unwanted sentiments. Tell yourself you can do it; if you haven't got your back, who else will have it for you? And never put yourself down. Recognise problems and try to fix them; mentally abusing ourselves has no benefit. Words are powerful and vibrate energy, even when said in our heads. Like attracts like; therefore, negativity attracts more negativity. So, speak prosperity into your life; it can only benefit you.

Have faith that good things will happen. One thing I've learned is to never give up hope. No matter the situation, always keep pushing for the desired outcome. In my 35 years, I've noticed that the universe usually provides a way through when we stay positive and don't give up.

Accept who you are. Acceptance is the first step in change. We cannot correct something we don't recognise as a problem. To change, you must know your faults and then take the necessary steps to fix them. So, accepting what is is the first component in progression. We can then work out a plan to correct our shortcomings.

Think long-term. Instant gratification usually comes with an unseen price. So, always remember the bigger picture of what you're trying to achieve. It's easy to get distracted by 'shiny object syndrome,' where we sacrifice the more important goal for instant fulfilment. But the ability to work now and delay gratification is the key to greatness. For example, if we wanted an incredible body, we'd have to put effort, work and time into it. We may have to sacrifice pleasures now, but that's what's necessary to achieve the goal. Nothing great usually comes quickly.

Balance is the key to life. Everything has balance and polarity; left and right are opposites of the same energy. The same essentially applies to good and evil. So whenever something terrible happens, understand that there is usually something positive that can be attained from it. It's up to us to look for or even create something good from bad experiences. If we master this, almost everything in life comes to serve us. We can learn vital lessons from unwanted situations and use them to propel us forward and not make the same mistake again.

What goes around, comes around. Whatever we create is like a seed planted that will grow into a tree. It's there to progress our creations into more incredible unforeseen energy. It will evolve and return to us advanced, to teach us something we can react to with even greater power. By universal law, every energy we create will return to us eventually. So always try to do good.

3

Actionable steps

Try to communicate with a confident demeanour. If we radiate the message that we're calm, confident, and know where we're going, people will believe that. So, keep your head up and walk with purpose. When dealing with strangers, most information is communicated initially through appearance. So if we radiate confidence and security, people will be less likely to want trouble with us. But understand, people possessing those qualities are more able to spot someone acting. But those with them aren't the ones to worry about, as they're more than likely of noble character. It's the troublemakers we want to believe we are confident, and they do not have a seasoned eye to spot what they don't possess. So always ensure to front a confident, assertive demeanour.

We all judge things by appearance. So, present yourself in the best way possible. From our clothes to our demeanour, they all play an aspect in fitting in. For example, we can spot police officers by their uniforms. In the same way, our presentation signifies who we are on the inside. The more comfortable we feel, the more confidence we'll radiate. These principles apply to more than just clothing. From how we walk to our facial expressions, they all influence how people perceive us. So always present yourself how you wish to be perceived.

Limit procrastination. If you desire something, seek and take steps to attain it. Life is precious and could end anytime; death is promised from birth. So don't waste time doubting yourself. Instead, know what you want and go for it; we only live once. If we procrastinate, the desired thing may no longer be available when we build the courage to acquire it. There's no time like the present.

Never be a people pleaser. Do things for the right reason, not simply to impress people. Doing so can very well cause the opposite. Everyone has a subconscious instinct guiding them, which follows the same laws as ours. Trying to impress people shows a lack of commitment to a more significant cause, as we try to get our fulfilment from their acceptance of us. People will distrust our integrity if we foolishly try to please them. Instead, we should inspire them with our actions of nobility and honesty; they will undoubtedly respect us more.

Do things right the first time. The time it takes to correct something to the level intended will substantially set us back. So, try your best initially, and then you can move forward confidently.

Learn to say no. We must say no sometimes; we cannot say yes to everybody. For example, imagine somebody wants us to help rob an extremely secure bank. That's undoubtedly a time a wise person would say no. Nevertheless, saying no is sometimes the best thing, so be ready to say it when necessary.

Keep it moving. If a stranger begs you for money or tries to distract you, don't stop. Instead, keep walking and give a brief answer like, "Sorry,

I'm broke," or, "I'm in a rush." Then, they'll probably leave you be. If you must stop, keep the interaction brief and then be on your way.

Practice makes perfect. We can master almost anything if time and effort are put in. Preparation is crucial for confidence. Mike Tyson was confident in the ring because he knew he had the skills necessary to win. If we practice something long enough, we'll get good at it. This applies to anything in life, being streetwise included.

Take as best care possible of your body. Our body is the vessel our spirit dwells in, and a bad vehicle will limit the driver's abilities. The better we look after ourselves, the more potential we'll have in all other aspects of life. So try to be as healthy as possible. People will naturally gravitate towards healthy-looking people as it's an outward statement of their inner will to be their best version possible. So join a gym, exercise, take up a sport or learn self-defence. It will surely propel your confidence and humility.

Be a trendsetter. Don't follow fashion because things seem cool. Usually, what is cool is the expression of someone who's decided to be unique. If we follow others, we'll never be first at anything. We live in the present, so every day, we have the opportunity to create new trends never before seen. Lead by example; others will believe in you and follow.

If you want to be the part, you must play the role. Whatever we desire, including being street-smart, we must start acting as someone who possesses what we want. If we take the actions required to become what we desire, we will slowly but surely soon be the real version of what we seek. For example, we must start practising if we wish to become great basketballers. Before long, naturally, we'll get better at what we've practised. This embodies the essence of making it until we've made it.

9

Teach yourself. Don't wait on people or the outside world to teach you what is right. Yes, we learn almost everything from others and the world around us, but remember to listen to your intuition. When fully mature, we must take all the things we've learnt whilst maturing and apply them to ourselves. If we dislike a learning experience, we should teach ourselves as if we were neutral within the development. For example, if we give someone of the opposite sex over-the-top attention and they give us an unwanted reply, don't be angry. Understand that it was simply them expressing what they felt was the correct answer to their emotion at that time. Instead, know that we all have the same inherent feelings dictating our actions, and if we were in their shoes, we'd probably do the same. Our aim, then, is to not create that unwanted emotion in others again. That way, we learn something positive from the negativity we actually initiated.

Break situations down. After experiences transpire, give conscious thought to the dynamics behind them. So, think, why did this happen? What could I have done differently? What can I learn from this, and what can I do next time? Doing this will naturally bring positive growth.

Having manners and respect is always beneficial. There's almost no situation where having respect won't benefit you. Everyone likes to be spoken to nicely, and doing so can save us from creating unnecessary problems. For example, someone could have a terrible day, and our disrespectful communication could be the final straw that makes them flip. Whereas kind words could've done the opposite. So always show respect, especially where it's due.

Avoid reacting with violence when possible. We can make disastrous decisions that ruin our lives in the heat of anger. Numerous people are serving long jail terms because they reacted in anger. And often, it's someone they didn't even know minutes before. They've now sacrificed their entire lives momentum over a stranger, which they could've avoided. For example, I'm sure someone out there had someone step on their shoe, react with anger, and an argument pursued. They then killed that person as a result. They would have moved on if they had kept calm and thought about what mattered. A life sentence in prison because someone stepped on your shoe is not worth it. So whenever we feel rage and want to react violently, we should always stop and think about the potential consequences. Then, we will likely realise it's much more beneficial to stay focused on our goals and not let others dictate our actions.

Limit letting your feelings control how you act. Emotion is essential in communication as it's a huge reason we communicate. It's the spark behind our actions, but we must also pair them with logical thinking for successful communication. Relying solely on emotion can be dangerous. You'll notice yourself performing at your peak in all aspects of life if you pair your feelings with unbiased assessment and conscious logical thought.

Be extra cautious when meeting new people. If you're meeting someone for the first time, always pay extra attention to assessing them. When approaching, survey the area to see if it's safe and if there are escape routes. Also, check if they have brought unexpected company. We wouldn't want to arrive to find them with numerous others and the ability to trap us somewhere segregated without an escape route.

Try to read body language. Most studies have found that over three-quarters of communication isn't verbal. Only 7% is in the actual words spoken. So try to read the non-verbal information people radiate. Our gut instinct plays a significant role in this. Study people's intentions in more than their words.

Don't boast. Let your actions speak for you, and focus your energy on the act of doing. Doing something productive is always better than talking about previous positives. Boasting doesn't make anything new. Instead, it's seeking rewards from impressing others by highlighting accomplishments. When we feel like boasting, it's because we did something we're proud of. That's our subconscious knowing that what we did was beneficial. Boasting polarises and neutralises that positive energy, and therefore the progression from it ends with the reaction to our boast. If we refrain from boasting, the positive energy we feel from recognising a praiseworthy deed can manifest itself naturally. And that's how that action we wanted to brag about evolves into a more decisive potential action to be reinvested into existence.

Handle your dealings in a place you feel comfortable. Of course, it's always safer to be in areas we know, as we know routes of escape or may have associates nearby. So, when possible, find safe, comfortable places you know well to handle your business.

Be wary if someone attempts to take you to a secondary location. Ask yourself, can the interaction not be fulfilled where you currently are? If yes, be concerned, as there could be a hidden motive behind their intention to change location.

Avoid over-intoxicated people. People severely influenced by drugs or alcohol can lose the ability to think logically or make intelligent decisions. In addition, they can misread things as their intoxication affects their perception. Sometimes they can quickly become confrontational. Trying to get an intoxicated person to think clearly can sometimes be impossible, so walking away is usually our best option. When we are forced to deal with a drunk person, stay calm and approach them in a friendly, non-confrontational way. Show genuine concern and move in a slow, reserved manner. Don't instruct them; offer them choices so they feel in control. If possible, help them find sober friends who they trust. But always walk away if it's a lost cause or they get violent; your safety is the priority.

Don't engage with crazy people. If you notice someone showing signs of insanity, avoid them. We cannot know their motive, and they pose a high risk of trouble. Even if they address you directly, a tactic they use for engagement, you should still take yourself away from the situation. And remember, mental illness isn't always noticeable, so be mindful to look out for the subtle signs.

Listen to your conscience and your gut feelings. Our subconscious is our radar, finely tuned into reality, alerting us to dangers and guiding us. It's the first thing our body suspects as truth from a combination of all our senses and all we know. It can notice things that our conscious mind cannot. It's developed over thousands of years of evolution, so pay close attention to it.

Don't be afraid to fail. Mistakes and failures are tools we learn from. Mistakes only lack value when we don't understand and grow from them. On the other hand, they become essential lessons if we ensure not to make them twice. Never blame failure on others if you are responsible for your faults. Blaming others is us deferring guilt and responsibility for our mistakes. And remember, only you can live your life; wrongly blaming others is ultimately unbeneficial. But, again, we must know the problem to fix it. So, when mistakes are made, accept responsibility, learn from them and take the necessary steps to correct them. The quicker we recognise problems, the sooner we can resolve them to achieve the desired outcome.

Accept when you are wrong. There's no point in trying to defend what we know is wrong. The time spent defending it will keep us away from the right path unnecessarily longer. So instead, accept wrongs speedily and take steps to find the correct route immediately. If we defend what's wrong, people will notice and lack putting their trust in us. If they leave us responsible for something, this shows them that if we make a mistake, we'll defend it rather than take fast action to correct it. Being wrong, accepting it, and finding the correct answer is vital to learning. And learning how to do things correctly is crucial in progressing all aspects of our life.

Be quick to listen and slow to speak. Sometimes, when we blurt out what is on our minds, we can make ourselves look stupid. Or even worse, get ourselves in trouble. So, always try to think before you speak and consider the ramifications of what you're about to say. We'll sometimes find that what we initially would've said was much better left in our heads. Also, listen attentively to not miss critical information.

Focus on the things you can change. There's no point stressing over the things we can't control. Spending hours being upset that it's gonna rain won't stop it from raining. But consciously accepting the facts and planning correctly to deal with that is best. So, in this example, find your best raincoat or umbrella and get on with your day.

Do the right thing. When young, we can assume that doing wrong is cool. It may seem cool to unwise people, but ultimately, people respect and follow leaders. And to be a true leader, we must have everyone's best interest at heart, not just our own.

Helping others can be beneficial. When we help others with problems, it's sometimes something we initially may not know how to resolve.

Therefore, assisting others in overcoming their issues teaches us valuable skills we could use if we find ourselves in similar positions.

Surround yourself with supportive and like-minded people. If we have constructive people around us, naturally, their positivity will affect us, even if it's just slightly. But more than likely, we'll attain valuable insights that can only benefit us. This is especially true if we interact with those ahead of us on our chosen paths, as they can teach us skills they've learned along their journey. But, on the other hand, if we hang with fools, we'll likely do foolish things. So, spend as little time as possible with people without decency or ambition.

Be genuine. Some people say fake it until you make it. I say make it until you've made it. What's the point of being fake when you can be authentic? Anything you desire to be, actively be that now. Before long, you'll become what you've been actioning.

Write goals down. Writing our goals down makes them over 40% more likely to be achieved. Having a list of realistic, accomplishable targets breaks down and visualises anything we aspire to. It gives us a clear path to success, as we know the tangible steps to achieve it. And then, we must work through them to reach our target. When we have goals, we have duties that keep us busy as we try to achieve them. And trouble is less likely to find us when we're busy doing something constructive. Predators prey on victims who look lost without direction, so having a path to follow is always beneficial. And if you don't write goals down, at least have clear, precise goals in your head. We cannot work towards something if we don't know where we are heading.

If you get arrested, stay quiet until you've spoken to a lawyer. Police can mislead people that talking is beneficial for them; sometimes, it sincerely isn't. Keeping quiet is perfectly legal, and it's wiser to speak with your brief first. Of course, we can always talk later after we know the possible consequences of our words. But remember, once you've told your lawyer something, they cannot legally withhold it. So also be careful what you tell them. Also, remember police will usually take the side of whoever acts the calmest in a neutral situation. Shouting or acting aggressively will seldom help.

4

Further principles

Do what makes you happy. Spending time going down the wrong path leads us further away from our desired destination. So, we should do our best to find happiness now. Everybody seeks happiness, and the closer we are to it, the more it will radiate to everyone around us. But, unfortunately, we cannot share what we don't have, so to be a leader and guide others, we must possess positive attributes.

Don't compare yourself to others. Everyone's path is individual, and we all advance at different rates. So instead, compare yourself to the previous you and continually develop into your best version possible. As long as we actively take steps in the right direction, there's almost nothing we cannot achieve.

If something sounds too good to be true, it may be just that. Always keep an eye out for things that don't seem realistic. Again, most good things don't come quickly. If they did, everyone would be doing them. Yes, sometimes we get lucky, and great things can be accessed easily. But for the most part, valuables have a price.

Always respect the youth. Yes, youngsters are learning, and adults have a lot more wisdom and experience than them. But we must respect the present-day youth. They encompass the current energy of life, and we can always take something from the upcoming generation. Moreover, even young children possess an innocence we can learn from. But, remember, youngsters have little life experience, and peer pressure and lack of wisdom affect their choices. How many reports have we heard of teenagers killing others over nothing? Literally, looking at them wrong or being from a different area are reasons youth have used to justify murder. So, always stay cautious; youngsters will do terrible things without considering the consequences.

Seek prevention rather than a cure. Suppose we can prevent something wrong from happening in the first place. In that case, it's always better than the negative thing happening and then having to fix it afterwards. So think long-term, and take steps to ensure the future is prosperous. Limit or eradicate instant gratification if it's detrimental to future prosperity. How many people are imprisoned with life sentences because they sought instant gratification? A lot. Yes, they may have experienced that immediate pleasure they wanted, but that's now just a memory. And now they must pay the price for the rest of their life.

Don't back down from stressful situations. Difficult situations teach us vital skills to evolve our skillset. We'll never learn or grow if we don't face challenging problems. Hey, even basic math was complicated for us at one point. But the key to growth is to push ourselves into the unknown; that way, we learn the skills necessary to overcome whatever challenges we face. Then, if something similar happens, we'll already have experience.

Understand that many people bluff. In the streets and life in general, people will try to call our bluff. Of course, it's not always the case, but remember that people sometimes bluff to win. So be ready to test people's sincerity, as they may not possess what they claim. But obviously, be cautious. For example, if someone threatens to shoot you, they may be lying to scare you. But on the other hand, they may indeed have a gun. So always practice caution when considering if someone is bluffing.

The dog who barks the loudest doesn't always have the worst bite. Usually, those who scream, shout and act pretentiously aggressive lack good fighting skills. Those who know how to fight don't need to flaunt it. Sometimes, the quietest in the room holds the most authority. So don't be afraid when someone shows erratic aggression flagrantly. They're more than likely unable to do much, so they express their scare tactics verbally and with gestures.

Hospitality isn't always the best. If someone or a group of shady-looking people ask you something frivolous like if you have the time, be careful. They may be relying on you pulling out your phone to rob it. So, sometimes be reserved when helping others, as we may be walking into their trap.

Effort and work will always lead to results. Every action has an equal and opposite reaction. So trust that every little detail you actively pursue in becoming the best version of yourself pays off. We may not notice it immediately, but by physical law, our actions will pay us in full.

Focus on doing and experiencing things. Actively doing stuff builds the skills necessary to propel at whatever we are practising. Yes, we can learn a lot from books etc. But, by taking that knowledge and practising it in the field, we develop our practical use of it and intuition.

As a human living in the present, there is always the potential to create life as we want. We have our creator in us and are the perfect vessel for the infinite spirit to be anything it desires. Understand we have no limits but ourselves. Don't doubt yourself; you can achieve anything if you do the necessary work. Have faith, don't give in, and you shall succeed. Universal law is law, and everything follows it. It's as valid as the Fibonacci sequence in nature. It's visible in the rising complexity of matter when sound vibrations pass through it. It is as perfect as math and has never let me down. So, trust in yourself to make life how you want it; only you can honestly do that. If we rely on others, our prize is not solely ours.

With transparency and assertiveness, we will almost always win.

You will become what you have been practising if you regularly practice these concepts. That's the operational aspect behind growth and evolution. We create our reality with our actions, and our actions stem from our thoughts. If you consciously control your life with a constructive mentality, nothing in this reality is unavailable. We can be and do anything we want. Being comfortable within yourself is the first step to freedom; from there, there are no limits but ourselves.

You may feel this information isn't relevant to becoming streetwise. But as someone whose seen all aspects the streets offer, these techniques are all pertinent to help us prosper on them and in every other part of life. Being streetwise isn't simply about being tough or scary. It's about being someone people respect and is based upon our ability to thrive in all situations we face.

5

Practical/brief techniques

- Keep your headphones to a level where you can still hear your surroundings if you're in an area where potential dangers may lay.
- Stay alert and aware of your surroundings. Try to keep your eyes up and on everything around you.
- Keep essential items with you. Things like a phone and money can be vitally needed sometimes. So try to be equipped for potential emergencies.
- Limit walking with coins jangling inside your pockets etc. It's a clear sign you have money.
- Use windows as mirrors to see your blind spots or behind you.
- Knowing self-defence is invaluable. Being able to defend yourself reflects the essence of having and not needing rather than needing and not having. Learning self-defence will always give you an upper hand in life.
- Look around before using cash machines or handing over large sums of money.
- Trust your instincts. Always listen to your gut feeling as it offers us information we cannot directly perceive. However, it's there to

guide you, so respect it.

- If someone bumps into you or brushes up close, check your pockets etc.
- Remember, there are evil people in this world. Never assume people are good-hearted. Many people have died because they trusted that a stranger had good intentions.
- Avoid hanging with the wrong crowd. Numerous times, people have been hurt or killed simply because of the company they kept. So, keep associates with a slighter probability of something terrible happening.
- Keep an eye out for shadows on the floor. They can be a great way to see if someone is sneaking up on us, as their shadow can sometimes be spotted before they get too close.
- When walking around corners, take the wide path to better view what is around them.
- If you're being followed, head towards a well-lit, populated place immediately.
- Limit walking and using/looking at your phone. This can be dangerous as you could walk into people, or even worse, traffic. However, if you must use it, regularly look up and put extra effort into assessing your surroundings.
- Safety in numbers. In some predicaments, it's safer to be accompanied by others. So, assess situations, and if necessary, take your friends with you.
- If somebody offers you something on the streets, it may not be what they claim. For example, someone may provide you with a cannabis joint. But it could contain anything, and they could be trying to spike you. So practice caution.
- Running away never loses a fight. Sometimes, running is the best option, especially if you're fast. It's better to run and survive another day with maybe just our ego hurt than fight and possibly lose our

life.

- Have your keys ready in hand when entering your car or building. This limits the distraction and time delay when entering. However, keys are also a possible weapon.
- If you have enemies, be ready to potentially cross them. Hopefully, it doesn't happen, but be prepared just in case.
- Try to mind your own business. Everyone has an agenda pursuing progression. It's always best to stick to our own path and not defer.
- Never flash a massive wad of cash in public. This makes you a clear target and can even tempt people to rob you who weren't even planning on robbing anyone initially.
- Avoid looking at strangers for too long. Staring can be rude, and doing it can cause unnecessary problems. So, assess your surroundings, but don't over-stare. If you get caught staring, politely say, "Sorry, I thought you were my mate."
- Stay in well-lit areas. Avoid going down dark alleys or dangerous or segregated paths.
- Make sure your shoes and attire are on properly to run. We wouldn't want to run, and our shoes fell off, or our trousers fell down.
- If you leave food or drink unattended, be cautious if you return to intake. Someone could poison our food whilst we weren't looking, and that would be our life over.
- Beware of people selling counterfeit goods. Usually, if someone is selling something incredibly cheap on the street, it's fake. Sometimes it's stolen, or the seller is highly desperate, but most times, it's simply not genuine.
- Assess elevators before entering. If someone or something feels off, don't get in. Also, immediately hit the alarm button and multiple floors if you're in danger.
- Park your car in a well-lit, safe area. Never leave valuables on display, and always lock your doors. Try and keep your vehicle in good

running condition. Plan and know your routes. Avoid hitchhikers.

- On public transport, keep your valuables close and hidden. Sit somewhere safe, like near the driver or women with children. If you are harassed, attract attention. Beware who gets off with you. Avoid falling asleep.
- If you are victimised, stay calm and alert. Note critical things you could use as descriptions, like the attacker's appearance and anything that stands out. Call the police immediately.

Remember, **YOUR LIFE IS WORTH MORE THAN ANY VALU- ABLES**. So, if it comes to it, always give up material items to save yourself from physical harm or death. We can always buy another thing. And even if it's something that cannot be replaced, nothing can truly be enjoyed without your health. So, never sacrifice physical health for material goods; if a robber wants it and threatens your life, give it to them. Unfortunately, numerous people have died fighting for valuables when they could've easily bought more. Don't let that be you!

Practice the principles detailed, and you will experience mature growth. You'll notice the world give you subtle confirmations you're acting correctly. Listen to them attentively. They encompass all the energy that's ever existed and are the universe's evolution progressing through you. After three to six months, reread these principles, and resolve whether you've been utilising them. Wherever you may be lacking, consciously try to grasp and practice what's missing. Anyone who masters these will ideally be an assertive, functioning, streetwise person.

If you found this book helpful, I'd be incredibly grateful if you could leave a favourable review on Amazon.

Thank you for reading, and All the best!

About the Author

Hi, I'm Daniel Jay Grossett, and I hope you enjoy this book and find it beneficial. I was born and raised in south London, and I lived in almost every area within it. I spent many years as a drug addict in and out of ten different prisons on forty plus occasions. Then, in 2020, my mother and best friend, Louise, passed away from cancer. That's when I decided I must change. I got clean, and then wrote a book about my life and all the crazy things I'd experienced over the years. Writing was a crucial part of my recovery as it gave me something positive to do, and knowing people would one day read my writing was enough to keep me going on the right path. Well, this is now book two, and I plan to keep at it if my books are received well. Anyway, all the best to you on your journey in life. Enjoy.

Also by Daniel Jay Grossett

Heaven or Hell-A True South London Story
The tribulating story of my life, where I went from being the smartest in school to a needle injecting drug addict. It contains all the crazy dramas that happened behind closed doors, the lessons I learned, and how I eventually got clean and turned it all around. It also contains things out of this world that you wouldn't believe was even possible, like how healed a hernia I had my whole life in under one year. Or how I interacted with entities not of this earth everyday for years. It's the unbelievable story of how I found heaven in my life, and how you can hopefully find it too.

Printed in Great Britain
by Amazon